Silent Nigh

A play

Colin and Mary Crowther

Samuel French — London
www.samuelfrench-london.co.uk

ISBN 978 0 573 12236 1

Please see page iv for further copyright information

CHARACTERS

Rose, 45, brusque, fretful
Wilfred, 50, worn, thoughtful
Lily, 20, fiery, spirited
Jack, 16, impressionable, confused
Peter, 50-plus, affable, firm

The action takes place in an Anderson shelter in a suburban garden

Time— Winter, 1940

PRODUCTION NOTES

The events in the play actually happened in the garden of a house which we once owned and were narrated to us by the man who lived next door to the family involved. Only the characters and dialogue have been invented.

The playing time is just 45 minutes, which shows how fast-moving it should be.

Despite being set in the war, it is easy to dress and stage. We believe its theme will speak to everyone's experience of the minor irritations and major niggles of living with one's family and its comic tone stops the whole thing getting too serious, whilst at the same time giving the audience something to think about on the way home.

Setting

UL we see an Anderson shelter, occupying about one third of the stage area. This can be presented as simply or elaborately as you wish. All that is necessary is that we see the back wall and a small side wall with a doorway in it, hung with blackout curtains.

There is a gap, C, allowing movement from one garden to the next, then a small section of picket fence to DR separating the two gardens. Just by the gap is a tin dustbin, its lid on the ground. The fence and bin lid are covered in snow. Inside the bin is a granite paving sett. (These days you can get them from any garden centre, for decorating your borders. In those days, they were still being used to cobble most road surfaces). At the back of the stage another length of decrepit fencing masks the base of the cyc, if necessary.

Inside the shelter, along the back wall, is a small bookcase, with a few games and books, an old cake tin, a tea caddy and a lantern or oil lamp. Next to this is a narrow bed. Bookcase and bed should look homemade, rough and old. Gasmasks in square cardboard boxes hang from a hook. There is an old gazunder beneath the bed.

Below the bookcase, to the front of the shelter, is an old striped deck-chair, with a footstool upstage of it. To the L end of the shelter, below the bed, is a small armchair or perhaps a Lloyd loom chair. Between the chairs stands a candle on a tin saucer, resting on a wooden packing case. There should be a box of matches by each light source, but both should be battery-operated for safety.

The shelter, like so many by this time, would be ankle-deep in water by morning and everyone avoids the walls, which are glistening with damp in places. It is a cold, dank place to spend any night, let alone one in winter. (To suggest the water, you could use a 3" high length of black wood to lie across the downstage and L sides of the shelter, so the soles of their shoes are not visible. If the audience will be able to see into the shelter from above, cover the floor with thick black plastic).

Wardrobe

Three characters are dressed in their night clothes. Wilf and Jack are in striped pyjamas and woollen dressing gowns and Rose is in a long, plain cotton nightdress and a candlewick dressing gown, with an old mackintosh over that. All three wear Wellington boots. Their clothes look crumpled, the men's hair tousled, Rose's in a knitted hat. They have clearly been woken up in the middle of the night and were more concerned for their safety than their appearance. The exception, in this as in everything, is Lily. She is dressed up to the nines, having only just come back from a night out. She wears a warm overcoat over her best dress. She wears full make-up, including deep red lipstick. Unwisely, she is still wearing court shoes. Obviously, she cannot afford stockings. (For Peter, see p.35)

Lighting

Lighting can be as simple or complex as you wish. Clearly separate the cold, dark area outside from the warm glow inside. You can recreate the air-raid on the cyc, but all that is necessary is a dull red glow, with one almighty flash, the glow fading as the night goes on. It should get noticeably darker just before dawn. When the lamp fails, do not be afraid of a very low level of light inside the shelter. At the end of the carol, an overhead pin-spot is needed to create the effect of a strange bright light, shining through a hole in the shelter's roof, as dawn comes up on the cyc.

Colin and Mary Crowther

To Jim for the story,
to Frank for his help with research,
and to that whole brave generation for teaching
us to stand up to a bully, whatever the cost.

Other plays by Colin and Mary Crowther
published by Samuel French Ltd:

Calling
Footprints in the Sand (Colin Crowther)
Just Passing
Noah's Ark (for children)
Reflections
Till We Meet Again
Tryst (Colin Crowther)
An Untimely Frost (formerly The Lost Garden)

SILENT NIGHT

A garden. Christmas Eve, 1940

The House Lights dim. Through the silence moans the wail of an air-raid siren. The curtain rises swiftly to reveal the garden on a cold, clear, winter night. Snow clings to a stretch of ancient picket fence, running from C *to* DR *and fills the lid of a tin dustbin standing next to the bin by a narrow gap between the fence and an Anderson shelter, which occupies the entire space from just* R *of* C *to* UC *to* UL, *to far* LC. *For full details of the set, see Production Notes. Distant fires burn fiercely on the horizon*

Wilf, Rose and Jack huddle, DLC, *frozen like rabbits in head lights, on their way to the shelter*

Wilf Wait. Wait for it.
Rose Jack, hold my hand.
Jack I'm not a child!
Wilf Steady. Run!

Wilf sets off at a run, crouched double, for the shelter

Jack Where's Lil'?
Rose Run, your dad said.
Jack She's not in her room.
Rose Nearly midnight and still not home! Just wait till I see her!

Rose and Jack run at a crouch to follow him, loaded down with paraphernalia. Rose carries her knitting bag, stuffed with all sorts. In her hands she carries two old knitted blankets and two old cushions.

Jack struggles with an old school satchel over his shoulder and two blankets and a pillow in his arms. When Jack reaches the middle of the garden, he pulls back. Rose sees the dustbin, its lid lying on the ground and full of snow

Jack We can't go without her!
Wilf Hurry up, you two — and bring that torch!
Rose Will you look at this? What have I told you? When you take out the rubbish, put the lid back on.
Jack There was no rubbish.
Rose You could still have put the lid back. Look at it! Full of snow!
Wilf Where's that torch?
Rose Jack! Torch!

Jack retrieves a torch from his satchel and passes it to Rose who runs to Wilf. Jack looks back at the house, assumed to be out over the auditorium, scanning it up and down for any sign of Lily. Wilf is largely unseen behind the edge of the shelter

Rose What's wrong?
Wilf Stuck, that's all.
Jack (*whispering loudly*) Lil'! Lily!
Rose Why you fastened it I don't know. No one's going to steal it.
Wilf I didn't want your hens getting in.
Rose They've more sense. Oh, give it to me.
Wilf Got it. (*He peers into the shelter through the blackout curtains*)
Rose Jack! Jack, get in here, now!

Jack runs over and is immediately arrested by the sight of distant fires. He remains URC, *watching the horizon*

Jack Wow!
Rose What's that smell?
Wilf Your bloody chickens!
Jack Ka-pow!

Wilf pushes his way, gingerly, through the blackout curtains, then wades across to the bookshelf where he attempts to light the lamp

Rose How deep's the water?
Wilf Three inches.
Rose Oh, good. Soon be having a bath in it!

Rose enters the shelter gingerly

Jack City centre, Dad. It's on fire!
Rose Has been all day.
Wilf These matches are damp.
Rose Oh, let me.
Wilf Miracle if there's anything left standing.

Rose lights the lamp, but the inside of the shelter looks even worse now

Rose Home sweet home!

Rose immediately begins making the place more homely, spreading her knitted blankets over the armchair and the deckchair and placing a cushion on each

Wilf I've told you before. I'm no builder.
Rose No, you're an engineer. So you should have known better how to hammer in screws.
Wilf Bolts.
Rose Same thing.
Wilf Not a bit like. I cut the tools that cut the metal into caterpillar treads for tanks. Precision tools. I do not churn out bolts and I certainly don't hammer the beggars in!
Rose Language. Where's Jack?
Jack (*imagining he controls an anti-aircraft battery*) Yack-yack, yack-yack, yack!

Rose hangs her knitting bag on the downstage back of the armchair then leaves the shelter. Wilf takes this opportunity to crouch down and open the cake tin. He takes a revolver, wrapped in a duster, out of his pocket and slips it into the tin

Rose That's next door's garden you're standing in!
Jack So are you!
Rose Can I help it if your father put the door on the wrong side?
Wilf I've told you ——
Rose (*to Wilf*) Save it for the angels. (*To Jack*) Inside.
Jack (*pointing* DR *to the house next door*) But, Mum, what about Aunty Enid, Uncle Peter? Margaret?
Rose Under their kitchen table. More fool them. And for the last time, we're not related.
Jack They're neighbours.
Rose Neighbours, not family.
Jack Next door neighbours.
Rose Wilf!

Wilf emerges from the shelter

Wilf Do as your mother says.
Rose Where are you off to?
Wilf I need to go.
Rose Should have thought of that before. Use the gazunder.
Wilf Oh, Rose!

Wilf returns to the shelter. Rose takes the blankets and pillow from Jack and passes them to Wilf who makes up the bed. Rose lights the candle and pulls out her knitting. Jack starts to follow

Outside, there is a muffled curse and a dishevelled Lily staggers on, CR

Lily Damn! I swear I'm going to chop that holly bush down in the morning.

Jack runs towards her

Jack Lil'!

Lily I've told you — don't call me that!

Jack Sorry, Sis.

Lily Or that. If that damned bush has snagged my dress, I shall personally ——

Jack Where've you been?

Lily If I told you, I'd have to kill you. In fact, I just might anyway.

The dull throb of low-flying enemy aircraft approaching

Jack (*laughing*) With that Billy? What d'you see in him?

Lily Wish I could remember ...

Jack Jerry's coming this way now! See that? *Messerchmidt*! They ride shotgun. Then come the *Junkers,* with all the bombs on board!

Wilf rises, selects a book from the shelves then returns to bed. He switches off the torch but keeps it with him

Lily Oy, Jerry! You're going the wrong way!

Wilf She's back!

Rose comes out into the garden

Rose Will you hush!

They all duck as the plane flies over. Lily is first to rise. Jack mimes drawing a gun, cowboy style and takes aim

Jack Bang, bang. You're dead!

Rose In — now!

Jack Ah, Mum!

Jack enters the shelter and puts his satchel on the bookshelves before crossing to sit in the armchair

Wilf Son.

Jack Dad.

Still outside, Lily is twisting to see the back of her skirt. She gives up and stomps downstage, towards the house, over the uneven ground

Rose Oh no, you don't! Get in here, where it's safe.
Lily All this and Mother too. Perfect end to a perfect Christmas Eve!

With a sigh, Lily gives up, turns round and makes for the shelter

Rose You've been drinking.
Lily Two bitter shandies. All night. Stingy beggar. Oh, and a sherry punch. Don't know what was in that, but I can tell you this, Mother. (*Suddenly sad*) It wasn't worth it.
Rose What wasn't?

Lily gives her mother a meaningful look, then heads inside the shelter

I knew it!

Rose follows her in. Lily kisses her father. Rose mimes bolting the door, then adjusts the blackout curtains carefully. Now, it all looks quite cosy in there

Lily Merry Christmas, Dad.
Wilf Hello, love. Nice time?
Lily Don't ask. (*To Jack*) Scram.

Jack rises and goes to the deckchair

Jack Not fair.

Lily collapses into the armchair

Lily I'm jiggered!
Rose Well you can be jiggered elsewhere. That's my chair.

Lily rises and makes for the deckchair

Lily Hop it.
Jack I never get a chair! I always end up on the stool!

Lily tries to examine the back of her skirt, but the light is not good enough. Rose picks up her knitting

Rose Now, perhaps, I can have some peace.

An aircraft approaches. They all freeze

Jack Gosh, he's close!

The aircraft is very close now. Wilf rises slowly

Lily (*rising, her attention on the floor*) Oh, no!
Rose (*rising*) What? What?
Lily My best shoes — wet through!
Rose Serves you right.
Lily Never let up, do you?
Wilf Not now, Rose.
Rose You never back me up!
Wilf I will when you're right.
Jack They're really close now, Dad.
Wilf Shut up, Jack.
Lily We don't stand a chance. Not in this tin shack.
Rose Should have dug it deeper.
Wilf I know.
Rose Three feet down, it said. Then cover it with ——
Wilf I know what it said. But at one foot down it was filling with water. At three feet we'd have drowned!
Rose Better drown than ——
Jack Dad!
Wilf (*rising angrily*) Shut up! Shut up! Shut up! It's my fault. Is that what you want to hear? I know it is. And how do you think that makes me feel, every time we ——

Jack Dad!
Wilf Will you shut the hell ——
Rose Language!

The sound of a terrific explosion, very close. Red light flares, with yellow, on the horizon, then dims. The dustbin falls over. Inside it is a heavy square paving sett. Lily screams hysterically. Rose rises, grabs the candle and flies to Wilf. The lamp goes out. Jack runs to Lily, clutching at her for support. They all cover their ears. Dust falls down on them. The candle goes out

Long pause in complete silence: no more planes, no more bombs, just the silence of eternity

Jack (*in a stage whisper, as if hoarse*) Dad!
Rose (*in a stage whisper, as if hoarse*) Wilf?
Wilf (*distantly*) That's it, then.

Rose breaks away. Jack comes to Wilf, who puts both arms round him

Jack Gone awful quiet, Dad.
Wilf Yes, well ... Lil'? Lily? Rose, help the girl!
Rose (*throwing out her usual practical challenge*) How?

Lily is in a bad way, rocking herself back and fro, whimpering. Wilf crouches in front of her, taking both her hands in his. Rose returns the candle to the packing case then sits, deep in her own thoughts

Lily Dad? I can't hear it, Dad.
Wilf It's the explosion, Lil'. Sent us deaf, for a moment. Be all right ... soon.
Lily No. The all-clear. I can't hear the all-clear.
Wilf There won't be one, love. Not this time. Not for us.
Jack Why not, Dad?
Wilf Ask your mother.
Rose Because we're dead.

Wilf rises and goes to the bookcase where, with his back to us, he re-lights the lamp

Jack No, no, Mum. Can't be. Not dead. I can still see you, hear you. You and Dad and Sis ——
Lily (*dully*) Don't call me that.
Jack I'll prove it. I spy, with my little eye, something beginning with W.

Without bothering to look up or round, the others respond robotically

Rose Water.
Lily Wellies.
Jack B.
Lily Bed.

Jack rushes upstage and grabs the round cake tin from the bookshelves

Jack T.
Rose Tin.
Wilf Don't touch that tin!

Wilf takes the tin and returns it to the top of the bookshelf

Jack Dad?
Rose Damn! Dropped one. No wonder, in this light.
Wilf Will you for God's sake stop that blasted knitting and do something?
Rose Like what?
Wilf Jack, light the candle.

Jack crouches and strikes a match, shielding the candle as he does so

Jack Not dead! I can still touch things — look — hold them, move them, light them, feel ——

Accidentally, Jack moves his hand at the side of the flame. Then he moves it away and moves it back again. He holds it there

Can't ... feel.

Wilf Lily, what time is it?

Lily Don't know. Watch stopped.

Wilf And mine.

Rose See?

Lily You needn't sound so pleased!

Jack Mum?

Rose Easy to prove one way or the other. Jack, there's biscuits in that tin.

Jack (*sitting on footstool*) Not hungry.

Rose Wilf, if you still need to pee, use the gazunder.

Jack (*jumping up*) No! Harold's in there!

Wilf Who the devil's Harold?

Lily His pet tortoise.

Wilf Don't want. Especially not with ——

Rose Lily, you've a smudge on your cheek.

Lily Who cares?

Rose considers their responses thoughtfully for a moment

Rose And for once, I don't fancy a cup of tea ... Anyone cold? No. Funny. Here we are, in a tin shack, at the end of our garden, in the dead of night, in the middle of winter, ankle-deep in icy water, in nothing but our night things ... and we're not ... cold.

Lily So?

Rose So ... we're dead.

Jack Dead.

Lily Dead and gone.

Jack But we've not — gone!

Wilf Not yet.

Jack We're still here!

Wilf (*shaking his head*) We only think we are.

Lily And when we stop thinking?

Wilf shrugs. Pause

Jack What now?
Wilf We wait.

Pause. Wilf sits

Jack What for?
Wilf Whatever happens next.

Pause. Jack sits on his stool. Lily holds out her hand. Jack takes it in his

Jack What's that, Dad?
Wilf In my experience — the bill.
Lily (*bitterly*) No such thing as a free drink.
Jack Sis?

Lily gestures despair

   But you must know. You taught Sunday School. You taught me.
Lily (*vaguely*) Clouds. Angels. Lots of singing. Hymns. Mostly hymns.
Jack Then what?

Lily spreads her hands on her knees, shrugs, looks down

   Do they have a football team?

Lily shakes her head

   Can I take Harold?
Lily (*evasively*) I'm sure they have ... pets ... cats and dogs.
Jack And tortoises?
Lily If there's room.
Jack I'm not going on my own.
Rose At this rate you won't be going at all.

Jack (*rising*) You don't know. You don't none of you know. (*To Wilf*) You don't believe it. (*To Rose*) You won't say. (*To Lily*) And you're making it up as you go along. It's like Father Christmas, all over again!

Wilf (*sighing*) All we have are pictures. No one's been and come back to tell the tale, so all we have are glimpses from dreams and visions: ranks of angels, golden haloes, everyone in long white ——

Jack I am not wearing a frock!

Lily (*lost in her own sadness*) Trouble with white, shows up every stain ...

Jack What if my friends see me?

Rose No chance. They'll be heading further south!

Wilf Rose! Look, Jack — imagine a great big house with room for everyone; wonderful party, everyone invited; but will everyone make it? Forget the details. Think how the picture makes you feel. That's heaven.

Pause

Jack And the other place?

Lily Flames and pitchforks are ... traditional.

Jack Eh?

Wilf I'll try again ... Pictures. Imagine that party — everyone inside, enjoying themselves — you, on the outside, looking in — on your own and knowing you always will be. That's hell: being left out, forever, and knowing it's your own fault.

Rose Where'd you get all this?

Wilf I talked to the vicar.

Rose When?

Wilf Last week. I went to see him about ——

Wilf gesticulates in Jack's direction, but so he cannot see

Rose Ah.

Wilf Poor chap. Been a bit down since his son was killed.

Lily Gerald. Nice lad, Gerald.

Rose You'll maybe get to meet him again now.

Wilf And Reggie ...

Rose Your father's brother. In the last war. Died when ——

Jack Never mind about them! What about me? What happens to me, Dad?

Wilf Ask your mother.

Jack Mum?

Rose My mother used to say that when you die you go up to the Pearly Gates and meet St Peter. He looks up your name in a great book. If he finds it, you go to heaven. If not, you —— don't. Comeuppance. Only right, Comeuppance.

Jack Why didn't you tell me?

Rose There wasn't time.

Jack You made time to tell me about Father Christmas!

Rose You were young.

Jack Why didn't you tell me about St Peter?

Rose You were too young!

Wilf Jack, Jack, it doesn't matter what *we* believe. You can't inherit belief, like blue eyes, or freckles. Something you have to work out for yourself, while you're young and healthy.

Rose And one day — pay for it!

Jack That's not fair!

Wilf That's life — or was.

Jack breaks up to the bookshelf

Lily I can't imagine life going on out there without me.

Wilf No more getting up on frosty mornings.

Rose No more cold feet.

Wilf No more feet.

Pause

Rose There'll be a lot to do. Funeral to arrange ...

Wilf Our lucky day. All four together. Might get a discount.

Rose Then the funeral tea ...

Lily Could try for the Church Inn. Function Room. Upstairs. Looks lovely, all done up for Christmas ...

Rose Who'll make the sandwiches?

Lily Aunty Enid.

Rose Who'll eat them?

Jack
Lily } (*together*) Aunty Jean.

Wilf Your Billy, he'll be there.

Lily Might.

Wilf Margaret.

Lily Might.

Wilf Your best friend — Margaret.

Lily Was. Till Billy came along.

Rose Who else?

Wilf Enid, of course. And Peter.

Rose Oh, yes, she'll be there!

Lily You've always had it in for Aunty Enid.

Rose She's just a neighbour.

Lily Next door neighbour. Lovely woman. Can't do enough for people.

Rose (*taking up her knitting*) No.

Lily At least she smiles and says hello. You, you don't speak to anyone!

Rose Keep yourself to yourself, my motto.

Jack Don't we know!

Rose You're not too old, young man!

Jack Yes, I am. And I'm not getting any flaming older!

Rose Language!

Lily Your trouble, you don't trust anyone.

Jack Not even us.

Rose And yours, madam, is you trust too easily. You'll learn.

Lily No! I won't! Not now!

Rose What's wrong with this family today?

Lily We're dead!

Pause

Rose Even so.

Wilf That's it, then. All over.

Rose Except for the will.

Wilf No need. All goes to next of kin. My sister.

Rose ⎫   ⎰ Jean?
Jack ⎬ (*together*) ⎨ Aunty Jean!
Lily ⎭   ⎱ Aunty Jean?

Rose That's what it says, is it, in this will of yours?

Wilf I ... didn't write one. Didn't think there'd be any need, not yet.

Lily But Aunty Jean!

Rose (*rising*) Over my dead body! Oh!

Wilf Oh, don't fret. She won't get much. House probably went when we did,

Rose wails. Wilf quickly backtracks

    Of course, it might not. Maybe just a part of it, like that house in the paper last week.

Jack I saw that! The whole of the front wall collapsed and you could see right inside, every room.

Lily I remember. Old dressing gown behind the door. Slippers under the bed.

Rose And the state of her front room!

Wilf There was a raid on. No time to go back and tidy.

Rose I'd have to. Dead or alive, I'd have to leave it straight.

Jack Wonder if they'll send a photographer?

Rose Who?

Jack Newspaper. To our house.

Lily jumps up with a scream

Lily My room!

Rose What have I told you? Time and time again? Clean your room!

Lily I was out!

Rose Gallivanting! Till all hours!

Lily And why not? Live life to the full, my motto.

Rose You wicked girl!

Lily I'm not a child!

Rose While you're under my roof ——

Lily News for you, Mother. We've got no roof!

Rose (*it suddenly hits her*) That'll be us. In the paper. Tomorrow! Our whole lives on show, for other folk to gawp at.

Rose and Lily sit, devastated. Pause

Jack (*coming forward*) All right. I've decided. I'll try heaven.

Lily No good. Got to choose while you're still alive.

Jack But I didn't know I'd had to. Not then!

Rose The ironing! I never finished the ironing! Damn! Damn and blast and ——

Jack
Wilf } (*together*) Language.
Lily

Jack It's not fair!

Wilf Son?

Jack It's all right for you. You've had your lives. They were nearly over anyway.

Rose Well, I like —— !

Wilf Hang on, lad!

Jack Mine's over — before it's even begun!

Lily Oh, Jack.

Jack And to think — I was afraid I'd be the only bloke going in the army next year without a girlfriend, or at least a picture of a girl to pin up in my locker — someone who'd write to me.

Lily I'd have written to you.

Jack Sisters don't count. Now I'm dead — and I haven't even lived. I've never had a whole cigarette — leastways, not one that didn't make me sick — or got drunk — or had a girlfriend.

Lily Had? We're not cream cakes!

Jack How would I know?

Wilf Son, the Seven Deadly Sins are not a menu.

Jack Pity. And I was so looking forward to working my way through them.

Rose I do hope no one heard that.

Jack I don't care! I'm sick of pretending — all everyone does in this country — pretend. "War will be over by Christmas". Wrong. "We beat those Jerries last time, we will again". Says who? They drove us out of France. Now they've bombed us out of our home. And you're no better. You never face up to anything. You hide away with ITMA and Henry Hall.

Rose At least they take your mind off ——

Jack The truth. It's time we stopped pretending. Time we said what we're thinking — what we really mean.

Wilf (*rising*) And what are you thinking, Jack?

Jack Thinking? I don't know! I wanted to grow up — join up — have mates — have some fun. Now it's too late!

Wilf puts his arm round his son's shoulder

Wilf Where's your sense of adventure, eh? Aren't you dying to know what happens next? Any of you? What the whole picture looks like when the last piece fits in place? What it's all been for? Where it's all leading?

Lily No.

Rose shakes her head. Reluctantly, Jack shakes his head as well

Wilf What a family!

Jack Sorry, Dad.

Wilf Ne'er mind. At least we're still together.

Rose For now.

Wilf What's that supposed to mean?

Rose Where were you Saturday afternoon?

Wilf Football.

Rose And the Saturday before that?

Wilf Football.

Rose Liar!

Jack (*sitting*) Sorry, Dad

Rose Jack was at the football. Only there was no football. It was cancelled. The men had fire duty. So Jack came home. You did not.

Wilf A man has a right to some privacy.

Rose Not from his wife!

Wilf Saturday afternoon is my time — for me.

Rose And who else?

Wilf What? Alone.

Rose On your own alone?

Wilf Of course on my own. If any of you had wanted to come, I wouldn't have needed to go.

Lily Go where?

Wilf If you must know, I'd take the bus to the terminus. Then I'd take to the hills.

Jack What hills?

Wilf What do you think those are — up there? (*He gestures* UC) The ones you could see from your bedroom window? They're called the Pennines.

Jack Can't say I noticed.

Wilf That's the trouble with the world today. No one bothers to look up, to look round, to ask why.

Lily What do you do up there?

Wilf Think.

Jack About what?

Wilf About life. About how we got here and where we go from here.

Jack And? What's the answer?

Wilf I suppose: we live, we do our best, we die. End of story.

Pause

Rose Is that it?

Wilf All right! I may not know about the next life, but I do know about this one. And I worked out why.

Rose Why you stayed away!

Wilf Why — though it got harder every week — I came back. Back to a wife who doesn't love me and, I realize now, never will.

Rose I never said I loved you.

Lily Mum!

Rose I washed for you; cooked and cleaned for you ——

Lily Oh, yes. Cleanest house in the street. But there's an awful lot swept under the carpet.

Wilf But I stuck by you. Because I love you, Rose. And it's why I always came back to a daughter, who, if her mother is right, is already three months gone and ——

Lily What!

Wilf If it's true, I'd be very sorry, but I shouldn't blame you and I want you to know I'd have stuck by you. Because I love you, Lily.

Lily Thanks, Dad. (*Glaring*) And thank you, Mother!

Wilf And to a son who worried me sick. Jack, I can't claim to understand you. I don't think you understand yourself yet. But when you did, I'd have stuck by you, come what may, through war and peace, success and failure, I'd have been there. Because I love you, son. And because that's what life — what love is all about — stickability. (*Pause*) I just wish I'd taken you with me, up to the hills, away from this smoggy town and out under a clean, grey sky.

Jack (*rising and hugging his father*) Thanks, Dad.

Rose reaches out and holds Wilf's other hand

Wilf Happy, now?

Lily You thought I was pregnant?

Rose I know men!

Lily But you don't know me!

Wilf returns to his book. Jack finds a sweet in his pocket. At first, neither of them seems unduly concerned by the row erupting around them, but gradually they look up and listen

Oh, Jack was right. It's time to have it out, Mother, once and for all. Let's take up those carpets and shake them on the line! Go on, then — bash away!

Rose Any minute now, that door will open and St Peter himself will call, "Come out, come out, wherever you are."

Lily No need — I'm already judged and damned — by you!

Rose Look at us — dressed for bed. Look at you — dolled up to the nines. In the middle of the night!

Lily I'd rather spend eternity in my best frock than your old nightie!

Rose You're shameless!
Lily Yes, I am!

Wilf closes his book

Wilf Lily, stop teasing your mother. What did happen last night?
Rose Jack, go to your room!
Jack I can't!
Lily Let him hear. He already thinks it. Thanks to you. Anyway, it's no worse than Billy thought ——
Wilf Billy?
Lily "Come to the dance," he said. Church Inn. Function Room. Looks lovely, all done up with a tree and garlands. I thought, tonight's the night! Especially when he said, "Come for a walk."
Rose Where?
Lily Down by the river.
Rose Where!
Lily I thought he was going to propose. "I've been keeping this warm for you, all night," he said. I thought it was a ring! "Happy Christmas," he said, and ——
Rose Jack, cover your ears!
Lily You needn't worry, Mother. I ran straight home. Home before midnight. For once.
Rose I didn't hear you.
Lily You'd all gone to bed. I sat in the parlour, looking into the ashes, and finally faced it. You were right, Mother. Right all along. Billy was never going to marry me. You should be very ... You and St Peter ... (*She starts to cry*)
Wilf Lily?
Lily Oh, Dad, I've sat and listened to them, one man after another, rabbiting on about themselves, thinking, soon, they'll remember I'm here ... But they only ever stopped talking to start ... When I said no, they'd drop me and move on, to a girl who'd say yes ... Oh, Dad, what's wrong with me?
Wilf Rose? Tell her.
Rose (*torn*) People talk.

Lily I know: I'm a disappointment. Always have been. Right from a little girl. I know you wanted me different. More like you.

Rose No. Oh, Lily, no. *Not* like me.

Jack Oh, you're not that bad.

Rose
Lily } (*together*) Shut up, Jack.

Lily Give me a hug.

Rose Magic word?

Lily Mum.

They embrace

Jack Can I have a hug?

Wilf No.

Jack Then bags I the deckchair!

Jack darts into the empty deckchair

Lily Sorry, Mum. Bags I the armchair!

Lily spins Rose round till the way is clear to the armchair

Rose Wha —— What's happening?

Jack We always say, if we have to spend the night out here, then halfway through we'll swap places, 'cos I always get the stool, Dad gets the bed, and Mum gets the best chair.

Wilf Take the bed, love.

Rose Cuckoos.

Wilf Eh?

Rose One day they just waltzed in out of nowhere, demanding food, thumping up the stairs, scattering ornaments — breaking the best ones — only ever the best ones, mind. And one day soon, they'd have waltzed back down again, slammed the door, and legged it, leaving the larder bare, piggy bank empty, and only a pile of odd socks to remember them by.

Wilf (*putting his arm around her, smiling happily*) Kids!

Rose Cuckoos.

Wilf goes to the bookshelves to check on the lantern

Jack What are they on about?

Lily shrugs

Rose (*to Lily*) I brought you up to stand on buses, let your elders sit
   down.
Lily (*rising*) Oh, go on.

*Rose nips behind Lily smartly and takes the best cushion then retires to
the bed. Her family spin round and stare at her, open-mouthed*

Rose No, ta. Just wanted my cushion.
Lily My God! She's got a sense of humour!

*Jack goes to the bookshelves and collects his satchel. Rose takes
advantage of his absence to take his place on the deckchair*

Wilf (*coming forward*) I think I'll stand a while.
Jack Me too.

*Jack copies how his father stands, with his arms behind his back, the
satchel still on his shoulder. Rose fidgets*

Lily Finish your knitting, Mum.
Rose No point. I realized ages ago: I've been knitting half the night
   and it hasn't grown at all. I just think it has.
Lily Knit, Mother.
Rose All right, Lily.
Lily Lily. What a name! No one's called Lily these days.
Rose I thought you'd like it.
Lily Why Lily?
Rose Family tradition. All the women in our family have always been
   called after flowers. My mother was Violet, her mother Rosemary
   — I think it was Rosemary. Might have been ——

Lily Couldn't you have found a better flower for me?
Rose Be grateful, You could have been called Rose.
Wilf Women, eh!

A companionable silence. Rose knits, Lily reviews her nails, and the men of the family stand on guard

Jack Daphne. That's a flower.
Lily Shut up, Jack.
Wilf Iris.
Rose Don't encourage him.
Lily I feel like I'm floating. Free. Free from all the fretting and planning; all the scrimping and ...

Pause

Jack We're still waiting.
Lily Perhaps there's a queue. It was a bad raid last night. All week.
Rose Perhaps they haven't made their minds up.
Wilf More like they're waiting for us to make our minds up.
Jack Perhaps they close for Christmas.
Rose Christmas! With all this palaver, it went clear out of my mind!
Jack Think of it! Turkey and all the trimmings.
Rose There were no turkeys to be had.
Lily You had a coop full of hens in that garden.
Rose We needed them for eggs.
Lily They haven't laid in months.
Rose They don't lay in winter.
Lily Then kill them!
Rose I thought we'd try something different this year. Got it off the wireless.
Wilf How "different", exactly?
Rose Mock turkey.
Wilf Mock?
Rose What you do, you roll out a ball of sage and onion stuffing into a sausage; wrap it in a piece of belly pork and pour gravy on it.

No one looks impressed

Wilf As well we missed it.

Jack I'll miss all my presents. You did get me some?

Lily Mum?

Rose Tell him.

Wilf We all clubbed together. Got you a bike.

Jack Oh, great!

Wilf Second hand, mind.

Lily Dad got it from the vicar. It belonged to Gerald.

Jack My own bike! Thanks Dad, Mum, Lil'.

Lily How about me?

Wilf Money.

Lily Perfect! I got you a packet of Craven "A". They're good for sore throats. Says so in the paper.

Jack I got you an IOU.

Wilf That's ... different.

Jack It entitles the bearer to have his boots cleaned — as often as he wants — up to once a week.

Wilf Thanks, son.

Jack Let's have a party. (*From his satchel he draws four paper hats, a bundle of motto-size pieces of paper*) Hand them round.

Rose Where'd you get those? Have you been rooting? I warned you no good comes of rooting.

Jack I made them, 'stead of crackers. This year I made new hats and new jokes.

They all don their hats with varying degrees of reluctance. Each one has been made from newspaper, but each is different, to suit the person wearing it

Lily Oh, good.

Jack No, they're smashing.

Rose That'll be a change.

Jack Why did the banana go out with the prune?

Rose I don't know. Why did the banana go out with the prune?

Jack 'Cos he couldn't find a date! And this one, this one!

Wilf Go on.

Jack What sort of cake do you eat in heaven? Angel cake! Hey, few
minutes more and we'll know if it's true ...

*They are all sunk in thought. Jack takes a paper wound-up whistle from
his stachel and blows it, sadly*

Rose I made you a ——

Her family speak absently, automatically

Jack Jumper.
Lily Cardigan.
Wilf Scarf.
Rose You don't sound very grateful. A lot of work went into ——
Lily We know, it's just ——
Rose Oh, don't spare my feelings!
Lily They're always a bit ——
Jack Tight.
Lily Under the armpits.
Wilf Even the scarf.
Rose Right! In future, I shall just sit here and do — nothing.
Wilf Don't be daft. You even knit in your sleep.
Rose We shall see.

Pause

Jack Holly. That's a girl's name.
Wilf Ivy.
Lily Oh, do shut up! (*To Rose*) I bought you a pair of stockings.
Rose Stockings? For me?
Lily Wrapped them, put them under the tree, before I came out. Why
I was late.
Rose How much d'you pay?
Lily Don't spoil it.
Rose How much?
Lily Three and eleven.

Rose How much? What are they? Silk?

Lily Rayon.

Rose But they're only one and eleven at Littlewood's!

Lily Which is why Littlewood's sold out.

Rose Then where —— ? Not the black market!

Wilf Where'd you go?

Lily Man with a suitcase. Corner of Market Street.

Wilf Ah.

Rose You can take them right back!

Jack Prob'ly not there now. After last night, prob'ly a great big hole there now.

Rose Serve him right! To think, a daughter of mine!

Lily The words you're looking for, Mother, are thank you.

Truce

Jack You know what I really wish for Christmas?

Lily Go on.

Jack A second chance.

Lily I'll second that.

Everyone gets tearful

Jack So why can't we have one?

Rose (*mumbling*) Because of me.

Wilf Rose?

Rose is clearly in great distress, gulping hard, breathing fast. Then suddenly she blurts it out

Rose I killed a man. Good as.

There, it's out. Rose sobs with relief while her dumbfounded children gaze on aghast. Wilf, however, moves to stand behind her, bows his head and places his hands on her shoulder

Jack Mum?

Lily Well? Did you or didn't you?

Wilf puts a finger to his lips. When the sobs have finished, and her children have stopped interrupting, Rose begins her story in such a light way it seems almost as if nothing matters now

Rose I was — oh, six, seven. Mother sent me to the stream for cress, watercress — fond of cress, she was — we all were — living on a farm, anything free was a bonus. But there was a man there before me — having a wash. When I got up close, I could see why. "You've missed a bit," I said. And he had. His arm, right up to ... He stood up, kind of helpless. "Are you bleeding, mister?" He shook his head. "But your shirt." Covered in blood, it was. "Won't come off," he said. And he smiled — raised his fingers to his lips, like — (*she demonstrates*) "Our secret," he said. Then he seemed to make up his mind. "Now it's your turn," he said.

Wilf withdraws his hands from her shoulders in horror

Lily Oh, God!
Rose I saw the cress — great green swathes of it, swirling in the shallows, getting closer and ——
Lily Mum!
Rose When I looked up, he was on the footbridge, looking this way, that, like he didn't know what to do, where to go. Well, he wouldn't. Not from round there. He looked at me, so I — (*she points to her left*). "That way." For I knew from Mother that track led to the road and the road to the town and the town to London, England, the World ... I watched him go, but like he couldn't see where he was going, or didn't care ... Then Mother started shouting. Where had I been all this time? I told her about the man and the blood — oh, and the knife I found in the shallows, all bright and gleaming it was ... Poor Mother didn't know what to think ... Till she found the body in the end cottage — newcomer — lived on her own, we thought. Wish I could remember her name. Can't seem to remember anything these days.
Lily Go on!
Rose Names matter!

Wilf Take your time, love. Take your time.

Rose Mother screamed for help. Father and the others came running. Only in the next field. Harvest, see. In the field all day and half the night at harvest.

Lily The point. Mother!

Rose Wanted to know which way he went. So I ... (*she takes the finger from her lips and points to the left*) He hadn't got far. Pity. I always dreamed one day I'd meet someone who'd seen London, England, the World ...

Wilf Breathe. Nice and easy.

Rose What a fuss they all made of me! Heroine I was. Till that winter. When they hanged him. Then it ... changed. If I went near, grown-ups stopped talking — children stopped playing — afraid I'd tell on them. Everyone's got a secret buried somewhere, see. In the end, things got so bad, we had to move. But the story moved faster. We moved again. In the end we came to Manchester. Moved next door to your dad. War on. People had other things on their mind. War over. Your dad came back.

Wilf Knew straight off she was the one for me. Loved her then — love her now.

Rose But I cost a man his life!

Wilf No! What he did cost him his life. What you did was right.

Rose Didn't feel right. All I know: I killed him. And now you.

Wilf No! A bomb killed us.

Rose But I didn't keep a secret!

Lily And that's what's been haunting you ever since? You were six!

Rose It was wrong!

Lily No! You were right!

Rose Me?

Lily Oh, face it, Mother, you're always right! You get everything wrong but somehow, somehow you're always right!

Rose Wilf?

Wilf nods

There's more.

Lily Oh, no!

Rose When we married, I determined. Only way to stop it happening again was to keep to myself. If you don't see anything, you can't hurt anyone. It worked. I began to hope. Then you came along. And the fear came flooding back.

Lily Is that why you never let me play out?

Rose Not so bad while you were children. I could watch out for you. But then you grew up. I couldn't protect you, from what they were saying — this time, about you. I tried to warn you, but you were too stubborn, too headstrong.

Lily Too like you.

Rose All right for Jack. He wouldn't notice a bad 'un if he fell over him, but you, you'd as like fall for him.

Jack Did you know this, Dad?

Wilf I knew there'd been a death and your mother was mixed up in it. Her parents hinted as much to mine. She wouldn't talk. So I filled in the blanks for myself. The way you do.

Lily You thought Mum had killed someone!

Wilf bows his head

Rose And still you married me?

Wilf Haven't I been trying to tell you for twenty-three years? I love you, you daft 'a'p'orth.

Rose Oh, Wilf!

They embrace, but she is still awkward in his arms and almost immediately pulls away. She addresses Wilf then her children

I'm sorry. So sorry.

Lily We forgive you. Though I can't speak for Enid or the rest of our neighbours you've snubbed all these years.

Rose I wish I'd been different ... more patient, more ... like the mother I wanted to be — not like the mother I had. Oh, why didn't I realize before? This morning when I woke. Every morning. "This day is so, so special. You can never have it again. So make the very best of it you can." It should blaze across the sky every dawn.

Wilf Maybe it does. We're just never up early enough to see it.

Rose I'm sorry. To Enid. Sorry to God. Sorry for calling you Lily ——

Jack Buttercup's a flower.

Wilf Daisy.

Lily Stop it. Both of you. Lily's my name. Mum chose it. Mum knows best. Though when I have a daughter ... if I'd had a daughter ... I think I'd have called her ... Heather.

Rose You didn't have to.

Lily No. I want to. I'm proud of you, Mum. Proud.

Rose Thanks, Lily. Now, never too late to make amends. It was a kind thought, buying me those stockings. But you're the one who needs them. I insist you let me pay for them. Jack, pass my purse.

Jack What do I get?

Rose You won't wear the frock, you don't get the stockings. Purse is in the tin.

Jack opens the round cake tin

Wilf Not that one!

Too late

Jack Crikey!

Lily What is it?

Jack (*showing her*) Looks like ... a gun.

Rose Gun? The boy's gone mad. Tell him, Wilf. Tell him it's not a real gun.

Wilf (*with a sigh*) It's not a gun. It's a revolver. Webley. Officers for the use of. My brother Reggie's. That and his cap. All we ever got back of him. Perhaps ...

Rose goes to console him

Rose No good comes of thinking, Wilf ——

Wilf Can't help it. Trouble with war. Makes you think. They're bombing us now, night and day. Softening us up. Come Spring, they'll invade. Nothing to stop them. Come Summer, we'd have heard them — marching over the cobbles, up Church Road — sharp right — knocking on our door — 'cept they wouldn't knock. Up to me then. No one else to protect you. And what could I do? I'm nobody. Got nothing. Only you. All the treasure a man has — his family.

Wilf catches Rose's eye. Now she understands. He speaks to her in the code that adults use in front of their children, however old they are

I'd never have let them touch you, Rose. Or Lily.

Lily's no fool. She grasps his meaning almost as quickly as Rose

Lily How many bullets?
Wilf Enough.

Lily gasps audibly and looks to Rose, who pooh-poohs the idea

Rose And where would you get bullets?
Wilf Man with a suitcase. Corner of Market Street.
Jack Can I see?

Wilf delves into his pocket. Then into the other one

Wilf Bugger.
Jack What? What?
Wilf Left them behind.
Jack Where?
Wilf On the mantelpiece. That little pot — with the seagulls.
Rose (*outraged*) That was a gift! From Scarborough!

Lily bursts out laughing

Wilf Sorry, love.
Rose You daft lump — I do love you!
Wilf Now she tells me!

They embrace, warmly and easily this time, and sit on the bed together, hand in hand

Jack Do you ever get the feeling they're not our parents?

Lily I've often wished they weren't.

Jack No. I mean, really. I do — more and more — I feel that I'm different — not like them at all — not like anyone.

Lily Oh, at last you've realized.

Jack I knew it! I knew there was something they hadn't told me.

Lily Could be. When you shrug like that and hunch and shrink inside yourself, you're just like ... like ...

Jack Like?

Lily Harold.

Jack My tortoise? I'm a tortoise?

Lily It would explain a lot.

Rose You're a good man, Wilfred. But I'm glad it didn't have to come to that.

Wilf Give me a hug. All of you!

Jack Oh, Dad!

Reluctantly, Lily and Jack approach. Suddenly, their parents dive for their original seats

Rose Bags I the best chair!

Wilf Bed's mine!

Jack They've done it again.

Lily So have I! (*She races for her chair*)

Jack is left standing. Rose laughs. She laughs and laughs. They all stare at her

Rose What? What you all staring at?

Lily You laughed.

Rose Well, and why not? No silly worries, now. With all that behind us, time to look forward. I can relax. Put my feet up. Here, I wonder what that St Peter looks like?

Lily Long flowing beard, like the pictures in Sunday School.

Wilf But you've never put your feet up. Not even when you had the influenza.

Rose Twinkling eyes.

Jack What's it matter what he looks like if all he's going to say is, "Had your chance, muffed it"?

Rose Jack!

Jack "Jack, you're a sinner." "But I haven't done anything — yet!" "No, but you wanted to." Zap! "Lil' — you're not." Ping!

Lily Thanks.

Rose It was a head cold. Now hush. If a soul can't enjoy her own funeral, what can she enjoy?

Jack "Mum, you're a sinner." "But I wasn't responsible!" "No. But you made life hell for everyone thinking you were." Zap!

Rose Well I'll be ——

Jack "Dad, you're a sinner."

Wilf I haven't admitted anything!

Rose Exactly!

Jack Zap! What's the point of justice when it comes too soon to say sorry and too late to make it right?

Wilf Jack, d'you really think he'd be able to enjoy that party he had planned, with only him and Lil' inside and the rest of us out in the cold? Course not. Soon as we'd seen the error of our ways — and we have, I have — and we came knocking to be forgiven, he'll fling that door open wide.

Rose Where's the comeuppance in that?

Wilf Do you want your comeuppance? Nor do I.

Lily Still, Mum's right. Not very final, this Final Judgement of yours.

Wilf There's only one thing final in heaven and on earth. That's love. And that is final.

Pause

Rose You've changed your tune.

Wilf Yes. I have.

Lily Let's hope St Peter agrees with you.

Wilf If he doesn't, it's my fault. Jack was right. I should have told you what life is really all about before it was too late to do something about it. My fault. I'll take the blame. I'll pay the price.

Rose You needn't think you're going anywhere without me.

Lily Or me.

Jack Or me.

Rose We stick together in this family.

Wilf All right. Tell him that. Where we go, we go together.

Jack I'm with you, Dad.

Wilf Lil'?

Lily Whatever Mum says.

Wilf That settles it. Now, when he comes, Rose, you speak for us. You go to church — you know your Thees and Thous.

Lily Agreed.

Wilf Tell him he can't split us up: we're a job lot. Up or down. In or out. Together.

Rose If you're sure?

There's a chorus of approval

Jack There's just one problem. What if ——

Lily What now?

Jack What if they're full?

Wilf Then we'll go round the back. Always room in the stable.

The lamp splutters and dies. They draw closer together round the candle. Pause

Rose Wish I could have said sorry to Enid.

Lily To Margaret.

Wilf Wish I'd made a will.

Rose Oh, let Jean have it.

Pause

Lily Who'd have thought the world could be so dark?

Wilf Strip away the tinsel and the carols, what are you left with? A
  family, in the dark, like most of us, with a candle, not knowing, just
  hoping, through the long and lonely night.

*Lily begins to sing "Silent Night". Slowly, the others join in, one by one.
The singing is raw, tentative, but above all hopeful, and by the last line,
the whole family has joined in, standing close together, singing in close
harmony, facing out, heads slightly raised*

*And as they sing, we become aware of a ray of light, shining through
what must be a tear in the roof of the shelter. At the same time, dawn
begins to break on the cyc*

> Silent night, Holy night!
> All is calm, all is bright
> Round yon Virgin Mother and Child,
> Holy Infant so tender and mild,
> Sleep in heavenly peace,
> Sleep in heavenly peace.

Pause

Jack Are we there yet?
Rose Wilf! It's started!
Lily It's getting lighter!
Wilf Can you see anything?
Jack Just light. The most beautiful light.
Rose Hush! Everyone — best behaviour. Lily, pull that skirt down.
  Wilf, hair. Jack — oh, why aren't you wearing your school tie?
Jack On top of pyjamas?

They crowd around the light, at the front of the shelter

Peter enters UL, *unseen, to behind the shelter. He is a small, rotund
man of late middle years, dressed in black trousers and worn braces
over a crumpled, white collarless shirt. Oh, and carpet slippers. And
if possible an ARW tin helmet*

Peter (*from behind the shelter*) You can come out now.

The family freezes. Frantic whispers follow

Jack It's him.
Lily St Peter!
Wilf Go on, love, speak up!
Rose What shall I say?

Rose addresses the hole in the roof in her best Sunday accent

Not at the moment, thank you. (*To her family*) I can't hear him very
well. Such an echo in here.
Peter Are you all right in there?
Rose Quite comfortable ... Much obliged.
Peter Are you coming out?
Rose Not till we know what we're in for.
Wilf (*to Peter*) Humour her.
Peter All right, Wilf.
Lily He knows your name!
Wilf Blast! Go on, what's the reckoning?
Peter How can I put it? There's good news and there's bad. Which
do you want first?
Lily Bad.
Jack Good.
Rose Oh, get it over with!

*Peter appears UR, on the far side of the shelter. He comes to URC,
pondering, then looks thoughtfully out over the heads of the audience
to their damaged house*

Peter Well, your windows are blown out, snow's blown in, fire's out,
back door blown to beggary ... What else?
Lily Did he say —— ?
Rose He's allowed.
Jack Then so am I.

Peter Oh, yes. Your chicken coop collapsed, hens everywhere, Margaret's chasing them now. Two are dead, but on the bright side, that's roast chicken for someone's Christmas dinner, lucky soul. More good news? Three have laid eggs.

Rose It's a miracle.

Peter Quite a few of those, this morning.

Peter walks to the gap in the fence and surveys the state of their Anderson shelter

You know, Wilf, you really should have dug that shelter deeper and covered it in turf, the way the Ministry said.

Rose (*glaring at Wilf*) Indeed.

Peter wanders RC *and takes in the fresh morning air*

Lily He still hasn't said — where we're going — where we are.

Rose Maybe he's building up to it.

Lily Can I try? Er, Peter, sir.

Peter Yes, Lily.

Lily Oh, you've heard of me?

Peter Quite a lot lately.

Lily (*pulling her skirt down*) All good, I hope?

Peter Depends who's talking. According to Mrs Harrison, her Billy will never walk straight again.

Lily Ah.

Peter According to Margaret, serves him right.

Lily (*to her family*) My best friend. Always said, best friend in all the world.

Peter Your question, Lily?

Lily Oh, yes. What does it look like, from where you're standing?

Peter turns upstage to admire the dawn sky

Jack Good one.

Peter Lovely. Sky all pink and gold.

Rose Gold? Sounds promising.

Peter Now are you coming out? Or do I have to come in there and ——

Jack I'd like to see you try!

Peter Ah, Jack. Might have known. Any final requests?

Jack Can Harold come?

Peter If he must. Anything else?

Jack I'm not wearing a frock!

Peter I'm glad to hear it. Now make your mind up, it's getting nippy out here.

Rose Nippy? As in cold, nippy?

Peter What did you expect?

Wilf Frankly? Something warmer.

Peter Enough of this. Are you coming out or not?

Rose Only if we can all come.

Peter Ah, yes. Sorry. Forgot. Enid says you'll not be feeling like cooking after a night in there — can't anyway — glass all over your kitchen — So how do you fancy breakfast with us? Only porridge and scrambled eggs — yours — but you're more than welcome.

Rose Enid?

Wilf Hang on ——

Lily Aunty Enid and ——

Peter Oh, and Jack. I'd be ever so grateful if you could remove a certain something on two wheels from my hallway. Tripping me up for days.

Jack Uncle Peter!

Rose Peter? Next door Peter?

Peter Who were you expecting?

Wilf You'll not believe this, but ——

Rose We'd be very grateful, tell her. Oh, and if she'd like a chicken to roast, we've got one spare.

Peter Thanks very much.

Wilf Peter, forgive a silly question, but what did happen last night?

Peter A bomb hit Church Road. The Inn took a fair battering. That Function Room will have to come down. Front's down already. Pity, looks nice, done up for Christmas. Man from the paper's there now, taking photos.

Lily Told you it was nice.

Peter Bomb sent cobbles flying everywhere. One went through the
    roof of your shelter, but you'll know all about that.

*The family, previously gazing up, now gaze down and focus on a large
cobble* DC *of the shelter, which, as it is mainly sunk in water, we cannot
see. Then they look at each other, as Peter rights the dustbin, peers
inside, and pulls out a large granite cobble*

I can see what happened here. One of those cobbles landed in your
    dustbin. Must have made a hell of a din.
Rose It did.
Peter Pity you didn't put the lid on, Jack.
Jack Eh?
Rose (*glaring at Jack*) Yes. Isn't it?

Peter drops the cobble back in the bin, where it clangs hideously

Peter So. Are you coming out? Or do I get her to plate it up and slide
    it under the door?
Wilf We'll, er, just have a quick wash and brush-up, survey the
    damage, then we'll be round.
Rose Wilf, there'll be nothing broken that can't be mended.
Peter Right. I'll go tell Enid to put the kettle on.

Peter makes for DR, *then stops and turns back*

Oh, knew there was something. Merry Christmas.

The others chorus "Merry Christmas"

Peter exits DR

Dawn lightens into day — a bright, blue, sunny new day

Rose Ready, everyone?
Lily Hang on, let me just ——

Lily gets out her powder compact

Jack I'm starving.

Wilf Dying for a pee.

Rose Wilf, perhaps tomorrow you'll let me come with you on that walk of yours.

Lily And the day after, Dad, you sit right down and make a proper will. No leaving it to chance next time.

Jack Or Aunty Jean.

Wilf But first, we're going to church.

Lily Together.

Rose I can wear my new stockings!

Lily I can feel my heart beat!

Jack We've got it — our second chance!

Rose Merry Christmas, Wilf.

Wilf Merry Christmas, Rose. Now. Are we ready to face the world?

Rose And start over?

Lily Together.

Wilf Right, Jack. Open the door.

They turn to face the world. As they do, quick

CURTAIN

FURNITURE AND PROPERTY LIST

On stage: IN GARDEN:

Anderson shelter with doorway
Small section of ancient picket fence. *On it*: snow
Tin dustbin. *In it*: granite paving sett
Dustbin lid on ground. *In it*: snow

IN SHELTER:

Blackout curtains hung at doorway
Small bookcase. *On it*: games, books, old round cake tin,
   tea caddy, matches, lantern or oil lamp
Narrow bed
Hook
Gasmasks in square cardboard boxes
Old gazunder
Striped deckchair
Footstool
Small armchair/ Lloyd loom chair
Wooden packing case. *On it*: candle on a tin saucer

Off stage: Knitting bag containing small, half-completed plain jumper,
   two old knitted blankets, two old cushions (**Rose**)
Two blankets, pillow, old school satchel containing torch,
   comic or book, paper hats, mottos and a paper whistle
   (**Jack**)

Personal: **Rose**: purse, handkerchief (in pockets)
Wilf: revolver wrapped in duster, watch
Lily: powder compact, handkerchief (in pockets), watch
Jack: sweet (in pocket)

LIGHTING PLOT

Practical fittings required: battery-operated lantern and candle

To open: Night sky. Effect of buildings burning distantly on cyc. Anderson shelter in darkness. Moonlight on garden, c

Cue 1	**Rose** lights the lamp *Cold light on shelter*	(Page 3)
Cue 2	**Rose** lights the candle *Warm light on shelter*	(Page 4)
Cue 3	Loud explosion *Vivid flash of fire on horizon. Lamp goes out.* *Cut warm light on shelter. After a pause, the* *candle goes out and the shelter is in darkness.* *Gradually fade light on cyc and garden over* *next five minutes until all is in darkness except* *for a low red glow on part of horizon*	(Page 8)
Cue 4	**Wilf** lights the lamp *Fade up cold light to shelter*	(Page 9)
Cue 5	**Jack** lights the candle *Fade up warm light to shelter*	(Page 9)
Cue 6	**Wilf**: "Always room in the stable." *Lamp splutters and dies. Cut cold cover in shelter.* *Gradually fade out red embers on skyline. Focus* *light on the family round the candle, rest of stage* *in darkness*	(Page 34)

Cue 7	As the family sings	(Page 35)
	Gradually start to fade up a very intense pink and	
	gold dawn on the horizon. Fade up pinspot through	
	hole in roof in very intense, very narrow beam, DC	
	of shelter	
Cue 8	**Wilf**: "Humour her."	(Page 36)
	Slowly fade up dawn cover on garden area	
Cue 9	**Peter** exits	(Page 39)
	Dawn brightens into day	

EFFECTS PLOT

Cue 1   To open   (Page 1)
           Air-raid siren, loud

Cue 2   **Lily**: "In fact, I just might anyway."   (Page 5)
           Sound of aircraft approaching

Cue 3   **Lily**: "... back where you came from!"   (Page 5)
           Aircraft flies over then fades away

Cue 4   **Rose**: "Now perhaps I can have some peace."   (Page 7)
           Aircraft approaching

Cue 5   **Rose**: "Language!"   (Page 8)
           Massive bomb blast very close, vivid flash of fire on
           horizon, dustbin, c, *falls over, then all sounds stop abruptly*